◆ ◆ ◆ ◆ ◆ ◆ ◆ ◆ ◆ ◆ ◆

EARLY
WILL
I SEEK
YOU

◆ ◆ ◆ ◆ ◆ ◆ ◆ ◆ ◆ ◆ ◆

Rekindling the Inner Fire Devotional Series

9703

REKINDLING
THE INNER FIRE

◆ ◆ ◆ ◆ ◆ ◆ ◆ ◆ ◆ ◆ ◆ ◆ ◆ ◆ ◆

EARLY WILL I SEEK YOU

◆

*A 40-Day Journey
in the Company of*

AUGUSTINE

Devotional Readings Arranged by
David Hazard

BETHANY HOUSE PUBLISHERS
MINNEAPOLIS, MINNESOTA 55438

Published by Bethany House Publishers
A Ministry of Bethany Fellowship International
11300 Hampshire Avenue South, Minneapolis, Minnesota 55438

Printed in the United States of America by
Bethany Press International, Minneapolis, Minnesota 55438

Library of Congress Cataloging-in-Publication Data

Augustine, Saint, Bishop of Hippo.
   [Selections. English. 1991]
   Early will I seek you / Augustine ; devotional readings
arranged by David Hazard.
      p. cm. — (Rekindling the inner fire)

   1. Spiritual life—Early works to 1800.
I. Hazard, David. II. Title. III. Series.
BR65.A52E6   1991
242—dc20   91–18871
ISBN 1–55661–204–4   CIP

To my father,

Wilbur ("Bud") Hazard

A long time ago you promised
yourself and your sons
into God's service.

Thanks for choosing the right path!

Thank you to the brothers at Holy Cross Abbey in Berryville, Virginia, for the generous use of their library.

Contents

Foreword

*O God, you are my God; early will I seek you!
My soul thirsts for you; my flesh longs for you. . . .*

———

Psalm 63:1

*O*n a sultry August afternoon, in A.D. 386, a
man named Augustine crossed an invisible boundary within his own soul. In a private garden behind
a Mediterranean villa, he fell to his knees and
ended a struggle between two voices that had been
warring within him for a long time, from almost
the moment of his birth.

Augustine was born in 354 in Thagaste, a village
situated among the vineyards and olive groves in
coastal north Africa. His father was a town coun-
cillor there, where the voice of pagan Rome still
ruled. In the temples, Man's flesh and sexuality
were idolized. In the schools of philosophy, where
patrician young men like Augustine were edu-
cated, Man's ability to reason was glorified as the
only pathway to truth, a good life, and happiness.

A brilliant thinker and orator, Augustine took
his place publicly among the leading teachers of
philosophy. With an appetite for fleshly pleasures,

he pursued a private life of sensuality. Both left him restless, searching.

But another voice called too.

Augustine's mother, Monica, was a Christian, and in her he saw ocean-depths of peace that spoke of another kind of truth. He knew only mental turmoil; something in her presence brought rest. He felt his flesh was burying him in lust; her life spoke purity and innocence.

At the pinnacle of his career, while teaching philosophy to the sons of the powerful and wealthy in Milan, Augustine privately concluded that these philosophies were empty, vain. And though he wanted freedom from the wearying demands of his flesh, he found he was trapped by them.

Augustine's conversion on that August afternoon was no calm, reasoned decision to "give Christianity a try." He sensed the bright-flaming presence of Jesus Christ calling him to follow a higher path. He ran from his villa into the garden, his soul in agony, tearing at his hair—"Going mad on my way to sanity," he later wrote.

In the moment Augustine "crossed over" the inner boundary—his human will—and consented to follow "the Way" of Christ, his world was transformed. He had held back a long time, but from now on he would hold back *nothing*. The living, real presence of Jesus became his inner fire, flaming out in all that Augustine would do or say from then on.

Augustine would become an influential bishop in north Africa: He would stand against creeping heresies that threatened to tear the church from within; he would brilliantly intercept the tottering Roman empire's threat of another persecution against Christians. To this day, his writings are questioned, diced, and minced for their doctrinal content.

I have come to Augustine to ask just one thing of him: *What did he know about the living presence of God—"God with us"—that made his own life flame so intensely?*

Augustine's writings challenge us by their spiritual passion and sheer honesty. Among the works presented here some are better known, such as the *Confessions* and *City of God*. Others are less known to many of us, such as his writings on the Psalms, the Trinity, the first epistle of John, and seeing God.

In preparing this book, which is for everyday use, I've used several sources. The phrasing is mine, as are the prayers that follow each entry.

In Augustine, I've found a trusted companion in the upward journey with God—trusted, because he is my friend and God's friend too. His honesty and love builds a fire against the darkness in me. His warnings remind me to seek God "early" in all my dealings.

I can think of no better way to introduce this new series of devotional books, "Rekindling the Inner Fire," than to invite you to take time over the next forty days, to travel in the company of Augustine.

David Hazard
June 1991

1

"What is scattered in me . . ."

Let all who take refuge in you be glad. Let them ever sing for joy. Spread your protection over them, so that those who love your name may rejoice in you. For surely, O Lord, you bless the righteous; you surround them with favor as with a shield.

Psalm 5:11, 12

*I*n all things that I contemplate as I am consulting you, I find no secure place for my soul except in you. And in you, I pray that what is scattered in me may be brought together, so that no part of me may be apart from you.

Sometimes when you are working within me, bringing my scattered self to you, you draw me into a state of feeling that is unlike anything I am used to, a kind of sweet delight. I know that if this spiritual state were made permanent in me it would be something not of this world, not of this life.

CONFESSIONS 10

My all-surrounding Father, how my soul is tempted to search for the meaning of my life in the love of others; to look for security in money and possessions; to strive for acceptance in service and good works.

Now I see how these can be temptations, open doors through which my spirit slips out from within your Self in order to trust in my own strengths. I close those doors right now, and place my soul inside your tender might.

Here, alone within you, I draw together all my concerns . . . all my responsibilities . . . all that is broken and scattered and needy. . . . My soul is fed and medicined with goodness from your hand!

2
"Late have I loved you!"

Keep yourself in the love of God.

Jude 21

Late have I loved you, O Beauty so ancient and so new. Late have I loved you!

You were within me, while I was outside of myself. I was searching for you in all the outward joys and beauties. And all I found was loneliness.

Then I fell and was broken by those same lovely things which I sought—things that you yourself made. Yet you were with me, while I was not with you. I was being kept from you by my hunger for the world's lovely things. I did not even recognize that all the things I sought had been created by Someone, or they would not exist at all.

Then you called me and cried to me and broke through my deafness! You sent forth your beam, the light of your magnificently beautiful presence. You shone your Self upon me to drive away my

blindness. You breathed your fragrance upon me
. . . and in astonishment I drew my breath . . . now
I pant for you! I tasted you, and now I hunger and
thirst for you.

You touched me—and I burn to live within your
peace.

CONFESSIONS 10

*My Father, the things that draw me
away from you, draw me away from my true self—the
self that can only be complete in you.*

*Little wonder then that on those days when I wander
far from you I feel "outside" myself. Isolated. Empty.
Distant and dark to all that I love.*

*Everything in me that is late to love you—today,
Father, touch it early with the full-dawning light of your
love!*

3

"Ascending" in the Heart

Blessed are those whose strength is in you, who have set their hearts on pilgrimage. As they pass through the valley of [tears], they make it a place of springs. . . . They go from strength to strength till each appears before God in Zion.

Psalm 84:5–7

*W*here do we begin our journey to God? How do we "ascend" to Him?

When we speak of our beginning point, the human tongue fails. Beloved brothers and sisters in Christ, please think on my words carefully, so you understand me. What I am about to say in reference to spiritual realities, I can only speak of in symbols.

When I speak about a "valley" it is a symbol of humility. And when I speak of a "mountain" it is a symbol of spiritual heights—that is, coming to a place where the high qualities of God himself become real in you. I don't mean for you to entertain an earthly image of valleys or mountain heights, for that will likely take you in the wrong direction, causing some to think of themselves as "higher" than others. Rather, consider Jesus.

Jesus, first, humbled himself. He descended to our earthly estate. In this "lower" life, we are all tempted constantly to live according to the flesh, tempted to base our thinking and actions only on what we can see and hear and feel and know with human senses. This is the lower estate into which Jesus came. By His obedience to the Father and His own suffering He entered into our "valley of tears." Only when we take the same position—obedience to God, patience in all that He leads us through—do we begin to "ascend" in Him. In lowliness we find our heights. Those who want to ascend to spiritual heights without passing through the valley of humility find themselves turned back.

Consider, for example, the two disciples who asked to sit next to the Lord in His coming kingdom, one on His right, the other on His left. The Lord saw that they were too quick to demand their reward. In their ambition to be honored, they were out of God's due order.

It was necessary that He turn them back to the place of humility until they could understand. So He said to them, "Can you drink the cup that I myself drink?" (Matthew 20:21, 22). For they were paying no attention to Christ's humility, wishing to reach only the spiritual loftiness they saw in Him—

or more rightly, the reward of honor they saw it bring to Him.

He called them back to the road as men gone astray—not to refuse what they desired, but to show them how to attain it.

HOMILIES ON THE PSALMS:1

Father, Son and Holy Spirit, all three— how can I even confess this, since you have poured out a Trinity of love for me? Here is the naked truth: My human soul shrinks in horror from laying aside its rights, wants, compulsions, demands. What if, in humbling myself, I'm set aside and forgotten? What if my wants are left hungering?

. . . No! This is only the voice of fear from my unbelieving soul. Never will I be forgotten or left wanting in you! Walking the servant's way toward your heights, I'll go from strength to strength.

I fix my eyes on the example of Jesus Christ, the high peak of my faith!

4

"Ascending" in the Manner of Jesus

Since we have a great high priest who has gone through the heavens, Jesus the Son of God, let us hold firmly to [actively walk in] the faith we profess. For we do not have a high priest who is unable to sympathize with our weaknesses, but we have one who has been tempted in every way, just as we are—yet was without sin.
Let us then approach the throne of grace with confidence, so that we may receive mercy and grace....

Hebrews 4:14–16

Where do we ascend?

As we've said, Jesus first descended to us, and He did this to show how we begin—in the "valley of tears," which is the place of humility. For us, it means submitting all that we *are* to God, receiving all that we *need* from Him, so that He can make us in spiritual appearance *like* Him. Fixed and determined in this attitude, Jesus lived His earthly life fully in the Word of God—abiding in the words that become rivers of living water to the inner man.

As it says, "In the beginning was the Word and the Word was with God, and the Word was God" (John 1:1). And also "the Word became flesh and lived for a while among us" (v. 14).

So it is by following Christ's example that our souls can begin their spiritual pilgrimage. Jesus is our "mountain of ascent": He lived fully in the Word of God, and in this way—by being humble before God—divinity showed forth in human flesh.

The Apostle Paul and many other saints have followed in these footsteps. Paul was able to ascend above all human weakness, above every worldly pursuit—all the things that will only be swept away by death in the end. He was able to live above all passing concerns by dwelling, in his heart, in a kind of state where the spiritual world—the heavenly City of God—and its rewards were always before him.

This was his practice, and in this state he heard with great joy God's "unspeakable [truths] that cannot be uttered" (2 Corinthians 12:4, Amplified). Thus Paul's inner man dwelled in the joy of God, no matter the outer state in which he found himself.

HOMILIES ON THE PSALMS:1, 2

My Father, where my plans are not your plans—oppose me! When a word on my tongue is not your word—silence me! Where I step outside your Word to struggle on my own, or to defend myself—draw me back inside of you.

Jesus, Word made flesh, you are the solid stone on which my soul stands. In your spirit of humble strength, I will be obedient and trusting of our Father.

Today, I lay aside all my natural powers, just as you did, so that the unshakable character of God may begin to grow in me.

5
That Your Soul May Live

*Listen! Listen to me [the Lord, your God], and eat
what is good, and your soul will delight itself in the
richest of fare. Give ear and come to me that your soul
may live. . . . You will go out with joy and be led
forth in peace!*

Isaiah 55:2, 3, 12

*F*inding the kind of life in which you are truly,
deeply happy does not come from anything we can
experience with the physical body. No, the kind of
happiness that comes through our physical senses
quickly passes and becomes just a memory, or else
it's forgotten altogether. Sometimes when I think
of base physical pleasures I once enjoyed, I'm even
filled with shame and loathing.

Nor does the happy life come from the mind.
For sometimes when I'm sad and I recall my past
happiness it only causes a melancholy longing—or
even frustration and anger—depending on how

difficult my present circumstances are. When even a true joy has passed, remembering it brings only sadness.

In neither the body nor the mind have I experienced the truly happy life.

How is it then, that I even *desire* true happiness? Where did the longing come from?

Far be it from me, O Lord—far be it from my heart!—to think that just any joy will make me happy with the heavenly joy you alone offer. I now know there is a joy that can never be experienced by the ungodly, nor indeed did I ever once find it when I was in an ungodly state.

Deep and lasting happiness is found only by those who cherish you, O Lord, for your own sake. Joy is *you*!

And the happy life is this: To rejoice *in* you. To rejoice *for* you. To rejoice *because* of you. I say it again: Life is joy in you, who are the Truth, O my God, the light of my soul, the health of my body!

Those who think there is a different way to find a happy life are pursuing something quite different from happiness—how sad that they do not even realize it. It's true they will find some "reflection" of joy. But they will not find the true thing, and in the end they will be sadly disappointed, as I once was.

The prophet Isaiah has said, "Seek the Lord that your soul may live." Yes—it is only when I am seeking you that your joy floods into my soul, giving happiness and health to my physical being as well.

CONFESSIONS 10

My Father, what a weak fool I would be if I continued trying to draw inner life from anything— from someone I love, from success in my work, even from spiritual service—other than you.

So I will draw life from these, your words to me: You call me beloved *in Christ Jesus. You call me* righteous *in Christ Jesus.*

High King of heaven, I am your child. And my brother is the Lord and Prince of all creation.

When I am restless, wanting something to make me "happy," I know this is your call to my soul. I'll feast on your Word, and find my life in you!

6

Living Among Those Who Dwell in Darkness

Woe to me . . . that I wander among the tents of [darkness].

Psalm 120:5

*T*he psalmist found himself wandering "among the tents of Kedar"—which signifies *spiritual darkness*. By this, he means to tell us that he was a spiritual man, the son of a bright, heavenly covenant, but that he was wandering among earthly and dark-minded people—perhaps even falling in with their ways.

Now this psalmist was a son of Isaac, the son of promise. And those who camped in Kedar were the sons of Ishmael, as we read in Genesis 25:13. These two sons of Abraham represent the two types of covenants under which people may live.

Ishmael was born of Abraham, yet he did not

28

receive the spiritual heritage. All those in the Church today who only know how to ask God for temporal happiness belong to Ishmael. Their worship is a carnal worship. Earthly blessings are all they seek—an earthly Jerusalem, an earthly Palestine, an earthly kingdom, an earthly salvation, victory over enemies, numerous sons, abundant fruits. One who has this Ishmael kind of faith will always be in darkness.

But Isaac was in the light. Isaac was not only a son but an heir to a heavenly kingdom. One who has the faith of Isaac is spiritual, wanting to advance in godly living.

Now these who belong to Isaac must still live for a time amidst those who belong to Ishmael. That is to say, even if you want to progress spiritually you must still live among those who are in earthly-minded darkness. If you are of Isaac you will try to ascend—to grow in the character of God himself (Ephesians 5:1). And those who are of Ishmael will try to knock you down.

This is a warning: If you wish to fly to God, there are those who want to pluck your wings!

I am saying—take heed!—that you must keep yourself from wanting to dwell among the "tents of darkness," because you will become just like them.

If you love earthly things, you wander far from God. Listen also to this warning: The body wanders in places; the soul wanders by affections. To love God is to throw off every spiritual weight that will keep your soul from rising to Him.

And how do we begin to throw off the weight of our fleshly life?

It is the practice of love—toward God and toward our neighbor—that keeps our soul from wandering, and from dwelling in darkness. The practice of love will bring us back, always, to the One who is Love.

HOMILIES ON THE PSALMS:7

My Father, I don't understand why you aren't answering some of my prayers concerning certain people in my life. There are those who need—and those who annoy. Why does your hand of change seem to move so slowly, or not at all? Sometimes I feel this dark-burning irritation. . . .

Or have I been wandering in the dark, seeking the wrong thing?

Lord, light the shadowy corners of my soul. Show me if the answer I want from you is something I want more than I want you.

7

"I approach food as I approach medicine"

Everything is permissible for me—but not everything is beneficial. Everything is permissible for me—but I will not be mastered by anything.

———

1 Corinthians 6:12, 13

For the fruit of the Spirit is . . . self-control.

———

Galatians 5:22, 23

You have taught me that I should approach the taking of food as I approach medicine.

For hunger and thirst are pains of a sort. They break down the body and burn, unless the "medicine" of nourishment relieves us. And it's by eating and drinking that we repair the daily losses of the body, until such time as you destroy both the stomach and food (1 Corinthians 6:13). At that time you will kill *all* fleshly hungers by filling us with your wonderful plenty. Then you will clothe this corruptible body with an everlasting body that cannot be corrupted (1 Corinthians 15:54).

But until that day—I fast and wage war because I need to bring my body into subjection.

Some do not understand how to fast, and so they fail. That is because they think only of the physical "ailment" of fasting. They think only of how uncomfortable it is, and they are lured by the pleasure that will come in breaking the fast by eating. And it is true that the "medicines" you give come through the comfort of your natural gifts, so that things of earth, sky and sea serve our weakness.

And that is precisely what I am coming to—our weakness. Our spiritual weakness is human delight. For while I pass from the discomfort of hunger to the delight of a full stomach—*in this very passage* there lie before me all manner of opportunities for greed and self-seeking evil.

Now, let us be honest, eating and drinking are pleasurable, and good food is healthful for the body. But I may sit down to eat and drink for the sake of health, and then for pleasure go on to eat and drink far more than I need or even what is healthful. Often, it is so difficult to tell the difference, whether my body has a healthy appetite, or whether I am being deceived by my own overwhelming greed, until I am seduced into thinking that I really cannot control my appetite. So then I

eat for the reason of gluttony and not in thankful-
ness to God.

Of course, my soul loves this state of uncer-
tainty. Yes, my soul rejoices when my true motives
are kept unclear. It loves to hide beneath the cloak
of "health" what I really want to do for selfish pleasure. Situated as I am among these temptations, I
struggle daily against sinfulness in my eating and
drinking.

I call upon you, O Lord, and offer up all my
confusion to you. Help me to clearly discern my
own motives. Because food and drink are needs *and*
pleasures, this is not the kind of thing I can re-
nounce once and for all, as I was able to do with
fornication. And who, Lord, is not sometimes carried beyond the bounds of "necessity"?

I ask you, O Lord, to help me keep a right grip,
neither too loose nor too tight, on the reins of my
palate.

CONFESSIONS 10

*My Father, show me where any of my
appetites are out of control.*

*Have I given in to a physical appetite for sleep or food
so much that it now controls my health, my time, my
demands on others? Do I hunger too much for perfection,
so that I become critical and dissatisfied? Do I hunger*

too much for affection, so that I dominate—or become overly pleasing?

Today, Father, I will be strong with myself—and honest. I will not call any drive a need, when it has grown into an appetite that takes over and becomes a demand.

8
The Origin of Evil in Me

I find this law at work in me: When I want to do good, evil is right there with me. . . . What a wretched man I am! Who will rescue me from this body of death?

———

Romans 7:21, 24

*M*y Helper, in all the ebb and flow of my mental struggles you did not permit me to be carried away from the faith.

This is my faith: You exist, and by your very substance you cannot change. You love and care for us—and you will judge our ways. So, in Christ, who is your Son and our Lord, you have established the way of salvation so that we can obtain the life that is to come when these earthly bodies die. And in the Holy Scriptures that have come to us with authority through your Church, you have verified and commended to us this way that leads to Life.

But even with these convictions, so safely settled in my mind that I know they cannot be removed—and even with the outer chains of evil broken—I burn to know one thing. What is the origin of evil that so often wells up from the hidden depths of my heart?

I have endured so many inner agonies to know this one thing. I have cried out to you, my God, with groans that came from my heart in its labor. I have begged to know, that I might be free. And even my agonized silences—the times when I was painfully sorry for my sin—were loud cries, asking you to show me, from a new depth of your love, the mercy that would release me from evil's bonds. In these terrible times, I spoke to no one else, not even my closest friends.

But all the time, you heard!

All of the "roaring and groaning" of my spiritual desire to overcome evil in my heart—this reached your ears. Because it was my heart's desire it was always before you.

Now I see that I was searching for the answer outwardly—trying to reason with my mind the best way to escape temptation—when the freeing knowledge I sought could only come by your Spirit as it brings inner light. As long as I kept struggling in this way, I was unable to return to the place where my soul might receive fullness and well-being and rest and joy.

But you, O Lord, who abides forever—you are not angry with us in our fumbling blindness. You are so merciful to "dust." It was pleasing to you to reshape the deformity that was causing my blindness.

You kept stirring me with the sense that I was missing some secret goodness that is in you. You kept me in a state of restlessness. Finally, I *saw*, inwardly, the truth about the origin of evil.

I saw how superior I felt, in my striving for spiritual well-being and sufficiency—but in all this striving I was still totally inferior to you. I'd been so blind to what I was doing, because pride is like a spiritual wound to the face, swelling shut the inner eyes of understanding. And through this swollenness of pride, I was groping and wandering and separated from you. But your healing hand applied to my eyes a stinging ointment that caused my pride and self-sufficiency to subside. What was this stinging ointment?

I was given a true understanding and sorrow for my sinful condition. And at the same moment that I beheld myself in this way, I looked upon you and your mercy for me. And you became my beginning point.

For you are my true joy! You are the Word made flesh, "the true light that illumines every man coming into this world" (John 1:9). I am subject to you! This is the right order of my spiritual relationship to you: That I remain inwardly gazing upon your image of love and mercy and strength, so that then by your grace I should rule over my body.

From that day to this, I have kept that wholesome sorrow for my sins—sorrow that causes me to run *to* you for the healing of my soul, and not *away* from you in my pride, mistakenly thinking that I can somehow prove my worthiness. For I see now that this pride—self-sufficiency before you—is the source of evil in me.

And so it is in coming to you daily—weak, hungry and in need of your Life flowing through me—that my troubled and darkened soul gradually gains in strength.

CONFESSIONS 10

My Father, you are daily making my mind to be "enslaved" by your law—the Law of the Spirit of life in and freedom in Christ Jesus! (Romans 8:1–9).

Today, I will not struggle vainly, trying to show you what a good Christian I am. At the very moment when I'm tempted and I want to hide my weakness from you— that's the very moment when I'll fix my eyes, instead, upon your welcome, your love, your firm and healing hand.

I will run to you for strength in the Holy Spirit. Clothe my weakness in your power.

9
"I will pass beyond the power of memory"

Since, then, you have been raised with Christ, set your hearts on things above, where Christ is seated at the right hand of God. Set your minds on things above . . . For you died, and your life is now hidden with Christ in God.

Colossians 3:1–3

Finally, brothers, whatever is true . . . noble . . . right . . . pure . . . lovely . . . admirable . . . excellent or praiseworthy—think about such things.

Philippians 4:8

How can I find you, my true Life, my God? Where shall I find *you*, since you are the One who gives me truly good and serene delight?

To find you, I must pass beyond this power

called memory—that is, my tendency to try to imagine you as being like any wonderful image I can call up in my own mind. Memory is a power of this lower realm. (Even beasts and birds have memories, otherwise they could never find their lairs or nests.) To find you—*you!*—who separated me from four-footed beasts and made me wiser than the birds of the air, I must pass beyond all mental images of you.

. . . What are you saying to me? That I must ascend above the reaches of my limited human mind to you who dwells so far above me. . . .

Yes, I will overcome and go beyond this power of memory in my desire to touch you at the point where you may be touched—where I may cleave to you. . . .

. . . I draw near to you now, sweet Light!

CONFESSIONS 10:17

*M*y Father, so often when I try to pray my memories weigh me down.

I carry the weight of insults . . . opportunities missed . . . prayers not yet answered . . . angry judgments . . . hurts and needs . . . the selfishness of someone I love . . . my own failures and sins. Rehearsing these things—the frustration, anger, or shame—crushes my spirit.

But today, I shake loose of memory! I set my heart and mind on things above, where you live—above the

40

limits of time, above hard circumstances. Fill me with your free-flowing grace and forgiveness that softens my soul and washes me free of the past.

    I will walk in your light, my Father!

10
"Going mad on my way to sanity"

Jesus replied . . . "You must be born again. The wind blows wherever it pleases. You hear its sound, but you cannot tell where it comes from or where it is going. So it is with everyone born of the Spirit."

John 3:8, 9

Lord, who is like you? You broke my bonds, and how you broke them I will now tell, so that all those who love you will say, "Blessed is the Lord of heaven and earth! Great and wonderful is His name!"

Your words had become deeply rooted in my heart, and I knew that I was surrounded by you on all sides (Job 1:10). I was certain that there was an eternal life, although I saw it "through a glass darkly" (1 Corinthians 13:12). I had no doubt that you were made of an incorruptible substance, and that you had created all things (Colossians 1:15–17). My old sinful life was tottering away as my heart was being cleansed of "old leaven" (1 Corinthians 5:7). And the Way—the Savior himself—gave me great delight as I thought about Him.

But I was unwilling to enter His narrow way. And it was becoming a heavy grief to me that I continued to act like a worldling, now that I longed for the sweetness and beauty of your eternal home. The reason for my unwillingness was that I was bound by my love for women.

Oh yes, I was certain that it was better to commit myself to your love than to give in to my sensuality. Still I kept giving the slow, sleepy reply: "Soon, Lord. I will come to you soon."

But "soon" had no ending. Because I was so violently held by my evil habit, my mind was being torn. I wanted freedom, but I was being held as if against my will—and I suppose I contributed to this state of confusion, since I willingly allowed myself to slide into sin.

But you, O Lord, used the changed lives of other men and women like a mirror to keep turning me around to face myself. You set me in front of my own face so that I might see how deformed, how crooked and sordid and stained and ulcerous I was. Horrified, I turned and tried to run from myself—only to find that you were there, too, thrusting me in front of myself. You wanted me to discover my iniquity and hate it, because it bound me and kept me from going with you.

Yet my soul hung back.

So I lived for a long while in a silent, trembling

misery, for I was afraid of giving up my sin as much as I feared death—even though it was because of my evil that I was wasting away to death!

Then one day, as I was reading the epistles of Paul, a great storm of agitation began to billow within my soul. My heart and mind and even my face became wild, as this inner storm built. There was a garden attached to our house, and I rushed out there so that no one would see me in such a wild state.

And there I was, going mad on my way to sanity—dying on my way to life!

My mind grew frantic: I boiled with anger at myself for not giving myself over to your law that brings Life. All my bones cried out that if I surrendered fully to you I would find myself free and singing your praises to the skies. I knew that it took but one step—a distance not as far as I had run from my own house to this bench where I had collapsed in my grief. To go over to your side, to arrive fully on your side, required nothing other than the will to go—but to will strongly and totally, not to turn and twist a half-wounded will so that one part of me would keep rising up and struggling, while the other part kept me bound to earth.

This inability to decide—for God or for my Self—was torturing me. I pulled at my hair, beat my forehead, locked my fingers together, gripped my knees with both hands. My whole body felt the agony of my desire to go over to you, but I could not will my soul to rise and cross over to God. I knew that what held me was such a small thing, and yet I turned and twisted as one held on a chain, as if my own agonizing might finally break it somehow.

Inwardly, I cried: "Let it be done now. *Now!*"

And you, O Lord, were standing in the secret places of my soul all along! With your severe mercy, you redoubled the lashes of fear and shame, so that I would not give up again, which would mean that chain which bound me from you would bind me more strongly than ever before.

I kept imagining the voices of mistresses, as they plucked at my garment of flesh, whispering, "Can you really send us away? How can you live without us?"

I ran farther from the house, into the garden, and flung myself down on the ground under a fig tree. Tears streamed and flooded from my eyes. I cried out, "How long will I keep saying, 'Soon' and 'Tomorrow'? Why can't I put an end to my uncleanness this very minute?"

And at that very moment I heard from a neighboring house a child's voice—whether a boy or a girl I couldn't tell—singing over and over: "Take and read, take and read. . . ." It was like the song in a child's game, but I'd never heard it before.

These words came into my heart with the force of a divine command: "Take and read. . . ."

I forced myself to stop crying and got up off the ground. I went back into the garden to the place where I had left the Scriptures, which I had carried outside with me—for I believed I had heard nothing less than a divine command to open the book and read the first passage I found.

I snatched the book, opened it and read the first passage my eye fell upon: "Let us behave decently . . . not in orgies and drunkenness, not in sexual immorality or debauchery. . . . Rather, clothe yourselves with the Lord Jesus Christ, and do not think about how to gratify the desires of the sinful nature" (Romans 13:13, 14).

I did not need to read further. There was no need to. For as soon as I reached the end of the sentence, it was as though my heart was filled with light and with confidence. All the shadows of my doubt were swept away.

CONFESSIONS 8

*M*y Father, you have given me your living Word and the inner fire-wind of your Holy Spirit. . . .

I bring to you what is still darkness in me.

Let your Word flame inside me with holy conviction! And let your Spirit's breath blow until the fire consumes my darkness and kindles in me your burning Light!

11
A Target for Evil

The Lord is a sun and shield; the Lord bestows favor and honor; no good thing does he withhold from those whose walk is blameless.

Psalm 84:11

As soon as a man wants to progress higher toward God in his faith—by this I mean, when a Christian wants to grow in the image of God by becoming stronger in His character—the enemies of faith will take aim at him. Their evil words will be like arrows shot at a target.

If you have never had to endure these evil tongues, then it is likely you have never really tried to advance in your faith. Whoever is afraid of what others will say will not even try to advance.

I urge you to set out for a higher point in your faith, even though you *will* become a target for evil words that are like the arrows of an enemy.

Before I say more about this attack, I want to show you a sure path on which you'll ascend to

47

a blameless faith. First, set your heart on attaining a closer walk with God. In your heart, decide that all earthly, fragile and temporal things are hateful if they keep you from progressing in faith. And get it fixed in your head that all earthly pursuits of happiness are "loss" compared to the surpassing greatness of knowing Christ Jesus our Lord (Philippians 3:7, 8). Set the eyes of your soul upon God alone. As you do this, you'll begin to find that a marvelous freedom comes: You are neither overly pleased by seeking earthly gains, nor upset when losses occur.

This is the point at which you find yourself being filled with the compassionate heart of God. As a result you will become uncomfortable with all excess goods and belongings that are hanging on you like graveclothes, smothering your soul. Suddenly, you will want to sell some of your excess and give to help those who are in need.

But when people around you see you gaining interest in a life that's pleasing to God—beware!—it's then you are in danger of the evil attack I have warned you about. The attack will come from those who will mock you for your "goodness." This type of person—a mocker—is a constant enemy of God and all that is godly. But this should be obvious to you.

I want you to beware of an even subtler attack that will come from false "spiritual counselors," those who turn you away from the path of salvation under the pretext of giving good advice.

You will know a true godly counselor by this: He will always point you toward the salvation of your soul, even if the advice seems unpleasant or hard. A false adviser will turn you away from the way of salvation I've just described and will offer you an "easier" path. Beneath a cloak of benevolence, a false guide is hiding a hatred and deadly rebellion against the Word of God. Though he seems to be making things easy for you, his words are killing arrows—and you are the target. So listen closely for treacherous words that seek to undermine your high goal.

One type of false counselors will say, "No one else is trying to live by these same high ideals as a Christian. Why should you be the only one?" You will recognize this type of "counsel" as an evil arrow because it seeks to turn you from the path by discouragement.

Another type of false counselor will seek to turn you away by praising your efforts. "Faith isn't difficult. Why struggle so hard? You've done so much already. Just rest." But as soon as you stop seeking to become like Christ, you begin to slip back into a worldly, self-seeking way of life. It will always be so, make no mistake.

Let any words that do not encourage you ever upward—toward freedom from this world—be put far from you. They are shameful. They are criminal.

Defend yourself from these words by being steadfast in prayer. Cry out to God, who is your shield: "Deliver my soul from treacherous tongues."

Homilies on the Psalms: 3, 4

My patient Father, you know that I sometimes get a burst of spiritual fire—that I often want to blaze into spiritual perfection with one amazing flare.

And then I go cold so quickly. I listen to unbelieving voices. And not all of them are "from without."

Only you—my steady-burning Light—can help me to be patient, committed, unwavering in my desire to love as you love. With all my heart I pray: Today, Lord. Just today!

12
Our Defense

I call on the Lord in my distress, and he answers me.

Psalm 118:1

*H*ow can you withstand "the arrows of the wicked" which I have been warning about? How can you defend yourself against the treacherous tongue?

Though the Lord defends you like a shield, He also gives you weapons which you can use to fight back. The enemies of faith may aim their arrows at you, but don't forget that you are also a warrior in the faith. The Lord has given you arrows to shoot, as well! As the psalmist says, "He will punish [the wicked] with a warrior's sharp arrows, with burning coals. . . ." (Psalm 118:4).

What is meant by this—"arrows" and "burning coals"? My children in the Faith, whom I so greatly love, please take time to meditate upon my explanation, until God gives you light and understanding.

A warrior's "sharp arrows" are the words of

God. When you "shoot" with God's words, and not your own, they penetrate the heart. When these arrows penetrate a heart they don't bring death, as our words will when we respond in self-defense and anger. God's words enter a heart when we speak them as a loving and gentle response, and they kindle life there. So we are to respond to faithless words with God's words, set on fire with love!

But what about the wounds that the arrows of the evil have caused within you? Make no mistake, when an evil word from a darkened soul is spoken to you—that is, a word that deflects you from the path of faith—it causes shadows to grow within. If you listen to darkened words long enough, you will give in to them. You will lose your way on the path, and begin to wander in a dark forest of doubt and fear and worldliness. It is then you must allow God's Word like flaming arrows to penetrate your own soul again.

Here are some examples of shadows that may grow in you, making a dark forest of the soul, shadows which God's true words must set to flame.

Some are wandering in this darkness: "Trying to live a life of faith is too hard. No one can do it." (If that is so, then why are others able?)

Or, as some say: "It's impossible to serve God when I don't have enough money. I have to think about my finances first." And some say, "When my health improves—then I'll be able to live for God." (Why, then, are there poor men who live for God? Why are there many who are strong in faith, though feeble in the body?)

And then, of course, there is this darkness—which has the appearance of humility: "I'm such a great sinner. I've sinned so much. . . ." (I would remind you of great sinners who have loved and served God more fervently *because* of all that was forgiven them.)

When we believe lies, I tell you, a baneful forest grows within the soul, and we become lost by excusing ourselves from service in God's kingdom. We allow ourselves worldly thoughts and worldly affections. The Word of God must come like a piercing arrow, bearing a flaming coal, so that this forest of worldly thoughts will be set on fire, become cleared ground where God may build His temple within.

The devil comes to sow tares and darkness, to bring ruin to your soul. The words of God come like fire, so that when your heart is cleared, Christ can be built in you, a temple of eternal happiness.

HOMILIES ON THE PSALMS:5

My Father, walk with me into the *"forest" of unbelief within. Help me to see where I have believed lies, letting them grow until they have overcrowded my path to you.*

Stumbling among my own doubts and fears, I can hear myself saying, "Lord, I can't. . . ."

And yet you whisper the truth to me: "But I can!"

13
Beholding the Image of God in the Inner Man

*[T ake] off your old self with its practices, and . . .
put on the new self, which is being renewed in
knowledge in the image of its Creator.*

Colossians 3:9, 10

*M*y friend, I have thought constantly about the debt that I owe you, since you are a devoted servant of God who asked me to help you by answering the question that was burning in your heart: How can we seek and behold God? I promised you an answer, but was delayed both by urgent business of the Church and because I needed much more time to reflect so that I might answer wisely.

I hope, now, that the Holy Spirit will help me as I write.

To begin with, I must tell you: The manner of

life you live, together with the state of your heart, is most important when it comes to this matter of learning how to behold the image of God in the sanctuary of your soul.

As we have all learned from our Lord Jesus Christ, this begins by learning to be meek. That is, we must come to Him daily for spiritual power and strength (Philippians 2:13). By seeking God's strength, not our own, we become humble before Him. Never allow any pride, which causes us to imagine and to pretend that we have no spiritual needs (James 4:10).

Let me digress for a moment to make a very important point about spiritual teaching. I don't want you to be distracted in any way as you reach for the high goal you long for so zealously.

You may read my words and any other spiritual writings, and you may hear many spiritual sermons and lessons. But words alone are not enough. Yes, it is true that understanding and sound logic will play a definite part in the spiritual life, but merely listening to all the spiritual teaching in the world will not help you nearly as much as the practice I'm about to recommend next. Therefore, think of spiritual teaching in this way: Teachers are the ones who sow good seed and water it; the rest is in the hands of God, who gives the increase within your soul (1 Corinthians 3:7). Your part is to diligently follow after Him.

Now I will tell you: You will make greater progress by secret prayer and meditation than by reading or hearing spiritual teachings. By these two crucial practices, you build up the inner man, receiving words of spiritual insight that feed your soul and renew it day by day.

Therefore, lift up the spirit of your mind, so that this daily renewing may begin. Set your thoughts on the character of God himself—think on the One who is full of compassion, kindness, humility, gentleness and patience (Colossians 3:12). Think on these things until you find yourself entering that secret chamber of the heart where Christ dwells in you by faith (Ephesians 3:17). Anyone may enter this place—there is no discrimination in Christ—whether Jew or Greek, bond or free, male or female (Galatians 3:28).

As you work at this practice you will find yourself growing stronger, even as "the outward man is corrupted" (2 Corinthians 4:16). That is to say, nothing that affects the outer man will be able to touch your spirit—not even weakness brought on by fasting, or illness, or physical accident, or even the onset of age (which is a fact of life, even for those who enjoy good health). If you do not let your inner man waste away by neglect, then you will grow strong and vigorous inwardly. Spiritually, you will never die as you learn, by prayer and meditation, how to become liberated from all exterior pressures.

If you want this kind of interior life, then pay attention to what I have just instructed you. And in this regard, I don't want you to depend upon

my authority alone, simply because this is something I am telling you. In order to act in complete
confidence in a matter, I want you always to base
your beliefs and actions on two things. First, the
authority of Scripture. Second, the truth that is
manifested to you inwardly, as the Spirit bears witness with your spirit (Romans 8:16).

ON SEEING GOD:1, 2

*My Father, I will quiet my soul now and
enter its "sanctuary" with you. . . .*

*When I listen to the secrets of my heart, I find that
my inner man is clothed sometimes with . . . pride and
an unwillingness to admit I've been wrong . . . impa-
tience . . . hard-heartedness toward someone who irri-
tates me . . . secret joy when another fails . . .*

*But today, Father, I will fix the eyes of my soul upon
you! Clothe me with your compassion, kindness, humility . . . so that others may feel even the slightest brush
of your garment as I pass by.*

14
Remove the "Spear"; Then Heal the Wound

Once you were alienated from God and were enemies in your minds because of your evil behavior. But now he has reconciled you by Christ's physical body through death to present you holy in his sight, without blemish and free from accusation—if you continue in your faith, established and firm, not moved from the hope held out in the gospel.

Colossians 1:21–23

Certainly, the renewal of the inner man that we are discussing is not accomplished in one moment of conversion. It is not like the renewal that occurs in the spiritual "baptism" that comes at the moment we receive forgiveness of our sins—the moment when all that stands against us is removed and nothing is unforgiven (Psalm 103:12).

It is one thing to recover from a fever, and another to regain one's health after the body has been terribly weakened by that illness. It is one thing to remove a spear from the body, and another to heal a nearly mortal wound by means of long and careful treatment. I am telling you that removing the cause is only the first step in the cure: This first step, as concerns the healing of your soul, is the moment when your sins are forgiven.

There is, in addition, the need to heal the spiritual illness itself. This is accomplished gradually, day by day, as you progressively erase the image of fallen man within and renew yourself in the image of God.

Both of these "operations" are set out in one verse of Scripture—Psalm 103:3. First, the psalmist refers to the One "who forgives all your sins." This occurs in our first baptism of God's mercy. Second, we read that the same One "heals all your diseases." This is speaking about the daily advances by which the image of God grows stronger in us.

The Apostle Paul spoke of this in clear words: "Though outwardly we are wasting away, yet inwardly we are being renewed day by day" (2 Corinthians 4:16). He tells us that this renewal takes place as we grow in the knowledge of God—that is, to meditate and fix our minds on God's personality, which is both just and holy (v. 17). By doing this, all that is false and temporary loses its hold on us, so that eventually we begin to resist and actually despise the things that lead us away from God's image.

This then, is the inner and progressive conversion of your soul—*to convert the direction of your love.* To stop valuing the temporal over the eternal. To stop trusting in the principles of the visible world more than you trust in the principles of the invisible world, which only makes sense to the renewed spiritual mind. Inward conversion means to stop spending all your energy escaping into pastimes that bring you fleshly, carnal pleasures in hopes that they will deeply satisfy, and to find that true lasting joy within comes from the wells of the Spirit.

It is only by constant effort that we control and reduce our desire to live according to the wants of our flesh, according to earthly principles. That means binding ourselves to what is *spiritual* by loving God and determining to follow after Him in spirit.

All our success in this, finally, depends on divine assistance. For it is God's Word that comforts and instructs: "Without me you can do nothing" (John 15:5).

This describes the daily process that takes place in those who are progressing spiritually as they should.

ON SEEING GOD:17

My Father, I don't want to continue to live as if I am still your enemy by being a friend to anything that pulls me away from you. And neither do I want to live as if you are an enemy to me, when you yourself have declared peace between us.

With your calming hand, help me to stop running from you. Soothe the "fever" that causes me to act like someone who is spiritually delirious. . . . Withdraw the wounding spear. . . .

Heal the disease!—which is the impulse to live as if we are still at war with each other, rather than living as Father and child.

15
God "With Us"

All things originate with Him and come from Him;
all things live through Him; and all things center in
. . . and end in Him. . . .So be it!

Romans 11:36, Amplified

What can possibly exist that is not *in Him* of whom this holy Scripture speaks?

It is only by the life of God that we, the living, are even alive. Likewise, it is only under the operations of God's great over-arching will that we are allowed to move and to make decisions (Acts 17:28). In this larger sense, no man is ever "without" God.

Yet, all men—and we ourselves—are not always "with Him" in the same sense in which God himself speaks through the psalmist, saying, "I am always with you"—and to which the psalmist replies, "Yes, you hold me by the right hand" (Psalm 73:23). Nor is God "with" all men in the well-meaning sense that you or I may have when we bless someone, saying, "The Lord be with you."

What I am leading up to is this: A man's greatest

misery is to be without God—that is, to have no inward connection to the One who is life and existence itself. Moreover, to have no remembrance that in God's original plan for man such a connection was possible.

When a man has no connection with God in this inward sense, he does not "remember" Him. So he does not seek to understand God and His ways, and does not delight in Him daily. As I say, he is not "with" God, though God be with him. (Be well advised and on your guard: There is even a state of forgetfulness so complete that it is impossible to be reminded of the One we have forgotten.)

To better explain what I am saying, and so you will not mistake this important point as something trivial, I will call upon an example from the everyday world.

Suppose you meet a man whom you don't recognize at all, and yet he says, "Oh yes, you know me." To remind you, he describes in detail where, when and how you met him. Yet after he's given all these clues you still say, "I'm sorry, but I don't recognize you." If he is correct, it means that other interests have so filled your mind you have forgotten him utterly, and that all trace of your former knowledge has been removed.

But suppose you finally do remember the man. Then you are returning to your right mind about him. Gradually, as you spend time together, you fully remember all that was forgotten. Not only that, you learn more and more details about him.

Now, consider the parallel I make with regard to your spirit—how you come to "remember" God, and how you grow in your daily walk "with" Him.

There are men and women, even in the household of faith, who are not "with" God. They do not realize that even the so-called good things and pleasant pursuits of this earth are really harmful when they cause us to forget Him. When we do not trust in Him, when we ignore or forget all that He is—then we are not "with" Him.

This is always to the harm of our own soul.

On The Trinity:12–14

My Living Father, each time I encounter you in a fresh new way I feel as though I'm rediscovering a part of myself that was lost, or dead.

What do you want to resurrect in me today?

16
Resurrection Faith

We fix our eyes not on what is seen, but on what is unseen. For what is seen is temporary, but what is unseen is eternal.

2 Corinthians 4:18

The Apostle Peter wrote: "Though you have not seen [Jesus Christ], you love him; and even though you do not see him now, you believe in him and are filled with an inexpressible and glorious joy, for you are receiving the goal of your faith, the salvation of your souls" (vv. 8,9). And the Lord himself said, "Blessed are those who have not seen and yet have believed."

So it is the matter of *belief* or *faith* that we must address.

The Scriptures are very important in building our faith. By their authority and testimony we are induced to believe. Whether we read them ourselves, or hear them read, they form pictures in our mind and, hence, we "believe" in what we have never actually seen except with the eyes of the spirit.

Consider our belief in the Resurrection of Christ. Though we did not see His actual Resurrection, we believe it because it was first testified to us. No one who lived at the time of Christ saw the Resurrection either. They only saw Him dying—but they believed firmly in the Resurrection because they later saw and touched a living Christ after they had known Him to be dead. These are the ones in whose testimony we trust. And as we read or listen to their true words, the Resurrection becomes real to us too in a kind of mental vision.

As we dwell on this mental vision, it becomes real and strong in us—we are almost able to touch it!—by faith. In this way, we become steadfast and firm in our belief in truths like these:

> Jesus Christ died and rose again.
> He was seen and touched by men.
> He now lives in heaven.

And, as the Scripture says, "We know that since Christ was raised from the dead, he cannot die again, and death no longer has mastery over him" (Romans 6:9).

No one living today witnessed these acts with their own eyes, but the power and the presence of the Risen Christ can be real within us—depending on the measure of faith we build.

ON SEEING GOD:8–10

My Father, I am so thankful that you have no beginning and no end! That you dwell outside the limits of time, in eternity. You know how easily I'm weighted down by the "urgent" things that occupy my time and keep me from living with eternity in view.

Create in me today a sense of your eternal life, goodness and love. Lift my sights above this thin, fragile, passing ribbon of time and set my foot on the solid granite path of eternity.

17
Why Some "Perceive" God While Others Do Not

O God, you are my God, earnestly I seek you; my soul thirsts for you, my body longs for you, in a dry and weary land where there is no water. . . . I think of you through the watches of the night. Because you are my help, I sing in the shadow of your wings. I stay close to you; your right hand upholds me.

Psalm 63:1,6–8

I'm sure there are many who wonder why they do not perceive God's presence with them, while others do.

It was Ambrose, my overseer and mentor in the faith, who gave me insight into this whole matter of our seeking God, and also the manner in which God reveals himself to us.

As Ambrose says, "No man has the power in himself to 'envision' God as He truly is. Yet there are situations that cause God to reveal something of himself to men—and to some men in particular, because of the circumstances in which they find themselves. In those cases, a man 'merits' a clearer vision of God because of the occasion. Then God reveals himself and it is purely an act of grace.

"And yet there is another matter here. Sometimes we do not merit seeing God in a difficult occasion, because we have not cultivated grace in our inner man. We have not sought God in order to grow in grace. That is to say, we do not merit the honor of being set by God in difficult circumstances—situations in which He wants to be made known—because we have not grown in our ability to see Him in our inner man."

By this explanation, Ambrose helped me to understand a matter in the Gospel which was unclear to me. He explained that God did not have two different intentions—that some should be favored in seeing Him, while others should not be favored in seeing Him. As the Apostle John has written, "To them that believe, He gave the power to become the sons of God" (John 1:12). These words, and something he wrote in a later epistle, apply to all men and women of faith: "We shall see Him as He is" (1 John 3:2).

I want you to notice that Ambrose was making a distinction. God will one day be seen clearly by all of His sons and daughters. But He is perceived today, in this world, only as He wishes to reveal himself—and then, only for specific purposes.

For example, God deigned to appear in the physical world to Abraham. When He did so, He chose to reveal himself in a very particular way that revealed some aspect of His nature, as befitting the occasion (Genesis 18). He appeared to Isaiah in another aspect of His nature, as befitting Isaiah's circumstances (Isaiah 6:1).

Yet He does not show himself so dramatically to innumerable others, even though they belong to His people and they are His eternal inheritance in Christ.

Nonetheless, in the world to come, all who are sons and daughters—all who have cleansed their hearts (Matthew 25:34)—shall see Him. Then, it will be His will to reveal himself as He is to *all*. And nothing whatsoever will block our vision.

On Seeing God:23

My Father, it's my natural tendency to seek you in the areas of my life where I'm in some distress. But you alone know what aspect of your nature I need to see today.

If it's your corrective hand that I need, help me to see it quickly and to respond with joyful obedience.

If it's your compassion, let me perceive how deep and

wide your love is, so that I can pour out that love on others, too.

And if your clear-bright purity is what I need to see, let me face it long enough that it cleanses away the sooty darkness that gathers so subtly in me. . . .

18
Becoming Clean in Heart

I care very little if I am judged by [any man or woman] . . . indeed, I do not even judge myself. My conscience is clear, but that does not make me innocent. It is the Lord who judges me. . . . He will bring to light what is hidden in darkness and will expose the motives of men's hearts. At that time, each will receive his praise from God.

1 Corinthians 4:3–5

*I*s it any wonder that the Lord is not made known in the present world, except when He wills? As Bishop Ambrose teaches, even in the Resurrection not everyone will see God, except the clean of heart. As Jesus Christ our Lord has said, "Blessed are the clean of heart, for they shall see God" (Matthew 5:8).

That means that some will never see God. We know that the unworthy will not see Him. For as our Lord said, "all who are in their graves will hear

His voice and come out"—but He made this distinction—"those who have done good will rise to live, but those who have done evil will rise to be condemned" (John 5:28, 29).

Without doubt, the devil and his angels are not allowed to see God at all, because they are not clean of heart. We must understand clearly what is written in the book of Job, where it describes the angels coming into the presence of God and the devil coming with them. We are not to believe that the devil saw God. They came into God's presence; He did not come into theirs.

Here is the distinction: When we see something, it "comes into our presence." But let us say that a man is invisible to us, watching us from an unseen vantage point. We may have a vague sense of "some presence," but have no idea at all who is watching. That hidden person, however, may observe our actions and understand what business we are about, whether good or evil. So our behavior and even, to some extent, the intentions of our heart are "present" to him.

In this same way, the angels and the devil came to stand before the Lord—but God was not before them. The evil do not want to see, indeed they cannot see God.

Therefore, what I tell you now is from deep understanding, important for us all: There are those who do not really want to see Him. As Ambrose warns us, "The man or woman who does not want to see God *will not* see Him. God is not seen in any place, except in the clean heart."

In saying that, Ambrose, who is a true lover of God, means for us all to take warning. If you will not devote yourself to the kind of spiritual work that it takes to continually cleanse the heart—that is, to free yourself from worldly thinking and pursuits, which result in spiritual darkness and fleshly lusts—then it stands to reason that you do not really want to see God.

But we are not like those strangers to God who live in this kind of darkness or in self-deception. We are the children who ask, and hunger to know, "How can we see God—how can we observe His true nature as it exists so purely in that invisible kingdom where His sons and daughters may look upon Him as He is?"

We are like the psalmist, who could say of God the Father, "He *will* satisfy my desire with good things" (Psalm 103:5). We are like Moses, who burned with such spiritual desire he cried to God, "Show me your glory" (Exodus 33:18). And like Philip, who longed with an inner thirst when he begged of Jesus, "Show us the Father and that will be enough for us" (John 14:8).

ON SEEING GOD:24–26

My Father, you see all—with eyes that are holy and compassionate. I know that you quietly observe me, even now.

Look into the depths of me, because you alone can

74

rightly gauge all that I need. That is, what should be corrected. Encouraged. Rooted out and destroyed. Or strengthened. I trust you to set aright the inner operations of my heart. . . .

19
Jesus, Image of the Invisible God

I pray that you, being rooted and established in love, may have power, together with all the saints, to grasp how wide and long and high and deep is the love of Christ . . .

. . . [so] that you may have the richest measure of the divine Presence, and become a body wholly filled and flooded with God Himself!

Ephesians 3:17, 18, NIV; v. 19, Amplified

*I*t is one thing to catch a glimpse of some principle or a single truth about God. It is quite another to take in His totality. This we do by building spiritual perception, so that we comprehend, more and more, the height and depth and great majesty of God.

When you see something so completely—like taking in the size, for example, of a simple ring upon your finger—then no part of it escapes your notice. Likewise, not a single detail of a plan that you conceive in your mind escapes your notice.

I use both of these examples because I want you to know how you may perceive the beauty of God. For we normally think of perceiving beauty with our eyes, but the beauty of God is in His complete goodness—consisting of virtues, or *high truths* that are all of His nature. These high truths—love, holiness, faithfulness and the like—we may look upon only in the depths of our soul.

Language limits us when it comes to talking about such deep matters. Our way of speaking limits us to talking about beauty in terms of form and color. But if there were not another type of beauty, spiritual in nature, then God would not be described as being "more beautiful than the sons of men" (Psalm 44:3, Douay Version).

The only begotten Son, who is now embraced in the depths of the Father, is the One who declares to your soul or mine the beauty of God. And He will speak to us in silence, from His Spirit to ours, in words that cannot be uttered (Romans 8:26).

At the present time, we are so limited by fleshly senses and rational thinking. But as we labor to become pure and holy in the inner man, we will become filled with the indescribable vision of God, which will one day fill us totally in that moment when we become like the angels.

ON SEEING GOD:21

My Father, I want to live in the beauty of holiness.

I want the sweet scent of Jesus Christ to be breathed into someone's life . . . a beckoning brightness to shine from your heart, through me, into someone's darkness . . . as we pass by together today.

20
Integrity

Have mercy on me, O God, according to your
unfailing love; according to your great compassion.
Wash away all my iniquity and cleanse me from my
sin. . . . Surely you desire truth in the inner parts;
you teach me wisdom in the inmost place.

Psalm 51:1, 2, 6

The condition of our faith is something that each of us must carefully examine. This can only be done if we are honest with ourselves and understand that no one else can carry out this spiritual work for us. Just as I can never truly determine the condition of your faith, so you cannot determine the state of mine.

"For who among men knows the thoughts of a man, except the man's spirit within him?" (1 Corinthians 2:11).

Some even want to prove that the wicked will see God. They wrongly believe that the devil himself has seen God. Because of this wrong thinking, they become confused when it comes to understanding the Scripture that says, "make every effort to live in peace with all men and to be holy; without holiness no one will see the Lord" (Hebrews 12:14).

I wonder how some can think that a man may allow wickedness to remain in his life, and yet he will see God. I wonder whether they think the devil (since he has supposedly seen God), is somehow following the spiritual path of a clean heart—that he "makes every effort to live in peace with all men" and that he is "holy."

ON SEEING GOD:11, 15

My Father, I want to become "clean in heart" toward everyone in my personal world. Give me integrity within.

Help me not to harbor judgment, while outwardly pretending that all is fine between us. Turn your search-light upon jealousy, envy, bitterness, resentment—any unholy attitudes in me.

Set me aright inside. Help me to live holy toward others. . . .

21
God "Appears" When the Time Is Best

I cried out to God for help; I cried out to God to hear me. When I was in distress, I sought the Lord. . . . Will he never show his favor again? Has his unfailing love vanished forever? . . . I will meditate on all your works and consider all your mighty deeds. . . . Your ways, O God, are holy.

Psalm 77:1, 2, 7, 8, 12, 13

*A*re you really willing to heed what it means to seek God, and then to hold on to a constant inner vision of Him? Then pay close attention to what I have learned, both by studying the Scriptures and by listening to wise spiritual teaching.

Ambrose has written to me, in his commentary on the Gospel, about this very important matter. To help me understand something of the purposes of God, he pointed out the occasion when the angel appeared to the priest Zechariah in the temple (Luke 1:11).

"There was an important reason," says Ambrose, "why the angel was seen by Zechariah, a priest, at this time, and also why he was seen in the temple.

"It was because the coming of our true high priest was near. Jesus, the heavenly sacrifice, was being prepared—a spiritual act of atonement and worship in which angels would minister.

"Take note, too," Ambrose urges, "that the angel appeared suddenly, so that Zechariah was startled. The holy Scriptures so often describe angelic and divine appearances as 'sudden,' and I believe there is a reason why this is so. It is because He wants to reveal with impact some new aspect of His plan or His nature. So in every sense of the word, that which was not seen or perceived before is suddenly revealed—and never to be forgotten."

Remember this, also. When Stephen was being stoned by the people he saw the heavens opened and Jesus standing at the right hand of God (Acts 7:55). And it was while mourning the death of King Uzziah, that the young Isaiah saw a vision of the Lord of Hosts for the first time (Isaiah 6:1).

God revealed himself to both of these men, though He remained invisible to everyone else who was present with them.

Therefore, we must always keep in mind that it is part of God's very nature to remain unseen—to keep both His will and His nature hidden from human perception—until it is in His perfect will to reveal himself to us.

On Seeing God:17, 18

My all-wise Father, sometimes I've asked for your hand to move, to change some circumstance—and have been disappointed that nothing has changed.

And sometimes I've sought you for guidance, only to hear in response—silence. Today, I gather all my scattered disappointments, confusion and unanswered prayers . . . and set them in your hands.

Renew me in joyful expectancy. I watch for your unfailing love to arise, as someone who has passed a restless night awaits the dawn. . . .

22
The God Who Is Always Near

I am with you all the days—perpetually, uniformly, and on every occasion.

Matthew 28:20, Amplified

The only begotten Son came to us from the depths of the Father's heart, and that is where He now abides. And He is the One who reveals the Father to us, because He is the Word made flesh (John 1:14) who dwelled among us.

So the transforming truth that is revealed to us does not come by merely listening to the Word of God, but as the Word is revealed by the Spirit of Christ to our minds (Romans 10:17). When the truth is revealed to us in this deep way it gives us a picture of God's very nature, which cannot be perceived with any eye. When we see the truth in this way, it can never be erased but continues to shine brightly upon all our innermost thoughts.

Those who yearn for this kind of spiritual light

within may take joy in this further lesson from my mentor, Ambrose: Our God fills heaven and earth (Jeremiah 23:24), and He is not limited to existing in some finite space. There is nowhere that He does not exist. He is completely present everywhere, but limited to no single place.

Whoever trains his mind on this truth will be carried beyond the boundaries of the natural mind, which so often "perceives" that God is absent. The man or woman who has not yet learned to escape the limits and weights of the natural mind should beg God's help in this—should seek God daily in spirit.

But do not "knock at the door" of other men for help in this. Men are only too quick to argue that God does not mean to be always present with us. Knock at God's door, for He will graciously strengthen you in the inner man, until you are able to find that He *is* with you.

ON SEEING GOD:29

My Father, you are never away from me . . . never forget me . . . never fail to surround me with your love. Where can I go from your Spirit? Nowhere— except in the doubts and spiritual blindness that make a cavern of my own mind.

Into those darknesses, bring the brightness of your presence now. Be the light that blazes in every dark doubt within me!

23
The Path of Love

*If I speak in the tongues of men and of angels, but
have not love, I am only a resounding gong or a
clanging cymbal. If I have the gift of prophecy and can
fathom all mysteries and all knowledge, and if I have a
faith that can move mountains, but have not love,
I am . . .*

. . . nothing.

1 Corinthians 13:1, 2

What is this kind of love, spoken of so highly
by divine Scripture?

It is the kind of love that causes us to forsake all
other ways of thinking and acting, and to pursue
what will be the highest Good for each man and
woman we meet. "Love" describes the activity of
one who has determined in his heart to be a lover.
And his love is not in word only, it results in loving
treatment of another person. So we have three
things that complete the circle of godly love: The
one who commits himself to being a lover; the one

he chooses to love; and the bright flaming force of love itself.

The carnal world sets its mind only on the attractive force of love—the good feeling it brings to approach love. It focuses on this power which unites two beings into one—or rather, *tries* to unite them—because this alluring, physical aspect of love will never be enough to complete the perfect circle of godly, eternal love, which never fails.

If we want to grow in the image of God, to go deeper into Him, we must make a distinction between this lower-world thinking and begin to seek a higher love. This we do by "ascending" in our soul, toward the place where we may drink as if from a pure and clear spring, from the source of Love.

This enables us to begin loving in spirit (when our flesh does not want to love)—for what is it that our soul loves in a friend, but the good things that we see in that friend? Here, too, we find the perfect circle of godly love: the one who chooses to love in spirit; the one whose spirit we choose to love, despite their outward appearance or actions; and the flaming force of godly love.

I do not say that, having caught a glimpse of this higher manner of love, we may then sit down and rest in our spiritual journey—as if, having seen it we have attained it. We have merely discovered, as seekers do, the place to look. We have discovered, not the daily power of this love, but only where it is to be sought. But that alone is enough to set us off on the journey toward a higher point.

There remains then, for us all, the ascent toward higher things—which begins when we decide to love as far as it is possible for men to love.

ON THE TRINITY:10

My Father, I confess that I have said of some I know, "impossible to forgive. . . .", or "hard to love. . . ."

I see now that I have sinned against you. Sinned against myself.

This moment—right now! before I think of one more excuse to remain sitting in this pigsty of unlove—help me to get up and make the first step on the road of love . . .

. . . which is also the highway to your heart!

24
Our Leader on All Life's Pathways

If anyone obeys his word, God's love is truly made complete in him. This is how we know we are in him: Whoever claims to live in him must walk as Jesus did. Dear friends, I am not writing you a new command but an old one, which you have had since the beginning.

———

1 John 2:5–7

[Jesus said], "If you obey my commands, you will remain in my love, just as I have obeyed my Father's commands and remain in his love. . . . My command is this: Love each other as I have loved you."

———

John 15:10, 12

I address this to each man or woman of faith whose spirit gives them the desire to seek the

"Fatherland." This visible world we now live in is, to us, what the desert was for the people of Israel.

Those people of old wandered in vain as they looked for their "fatherland"—but in the times when they let the Father himself be their guide, they made progress and did not lose their way. The reason they so often lost their way again was because they did not distinguish between the geographical path and the spiritual way.

God's "way" for those people, in that day, was obedience to His commandments. Because they overlooked or ignored the spiritual path, they never attained the land where they would have found the blessing and rest they wanted.

It is important for us to think on this: The people of Israel were lost for forty years on a path which normally takes only weeks to cross and was already known to them besides. And they were delayed, not because God had abandoned them, but because they were being tried and purified.

By that, I mean to remind you that God has promised us ineffable sweetness and goodness. As I have so often taught you, quoting the Scriptures, "No eye has seen, no ear has heard, no mind has conceived what God has prepared for those who love him" (1 Corinthians 2:9). But so often, we allow ourselves to be sidetracked from following Him because we focus our attention on temporal affairs. We let the world tempt us with what is "good" according to its evil standards, and even as believers we forget that we are on a spiritual pilgrimage.

If you don't want to die of thirst in the desert of this world, let your soul drink of God's love. This is the fountain God has chosen to place here in this world, to keep us from fainting on our way home to Him.

Be assured, if there is one fountain we will drink from abundantly when we finally reach our "Fatherland," it will be the fountain of God's love.

HOMILIES ON THE FIRST EPISTLE OF JOHN:1

My Father, open the eyes of my soul. Cause me to see that any issue that causes distrust or anger between me and another . . . even my own iron "rightness" on matters of faith . . . can cause me to make a desert "in the name of the Lord."

I thirst to be like you . . . patient and kind . . . not proud or rude . . . not easily angered . . .

. . . keeping no record of wrongs. . . .

25
Living in the "Light" With Each Other

Whoever loves his brother lives in the light, and there is nothing in him to make him stumble.

1 John 2:10

*B*y elevating the kind of life that's based upon love for our brothers, it is clear that the Apostle John is making this statement: Our right standing with God is shown as we come to love our brothers, and we ourselves enjoy more perfect spiritual freedom as well. When we harbor no hidden sin against others, it's then that God's light will shine more clearly and perfectly within us, so we are not stumbling in darkness. It is interesting to me that John apparently includes God in this statement, both as a "brother" whom we must love, and one with whom we must live in the light.

Further on in John's epistle, he emphasizes:

"Dear friends, let us love one another, for love comes from God. Everyone who loves has been born of God and knows God. Whoever does not love does not know God, for God is love" (1 John 4:7, 8).

We should take note of the truth that is being revealed to us, by no less an authority than one of the apostles. This very love—simple brotherly love, which we may easily have for one another—is not merely "from" God. It works within us, transforming us into the living image of God.

So, we must remember two things on this first point. When love causes us to act with grace and charity toward someone, it is not simply flowing from our own human heart—it is from God! And therefore, it should be our goal to grow in love for each other.

Still later we read, "If anyone says, 'I love God,' yet hates his brother, he is a liar. For anyone who does not love his brother, whom he has seen, cannot love God, whom he has not seen" (1 John 4:20). The fact that he does not love his brother is the very reason that he cannot see God.

With our human sight, we are only able to perceive flesh-and-blood men and women. The kind of sight needed to perceive God is something altogether different, since He is invisible to the human eye. But when we love our brother, with this true spiritual love we are talking about, then we begin to experience inwardly the ability to see God.

As the Scripture is telling us, God is love itself.

When we love we discover, growing within us, the ability to see with the eyes of the inner man. This is the only kind of sight whereby we can begin to see God at all.

ON THE TRINITY:8

My Father, you know there is one whom I "stumble" over time and again. Sometimes the best I can do is pretend to love . . . and then keep my distance. . . .

Take me the next step, Father. And give me your grace—your unfailing ability—to act in real love.

26
Our Great Debt Is Forgiven

Our Father in heaven, . . . Forgive us our debts, as we also have forgiven our debtors.

Matthew 6:9, 12

What do you suppose I am going to talk to you about, after reading this Scripture—except love? Many of us are blind to the fact that forgiveness is the tool of love, in this present world.

Indeed, we Christians have made a contract with God in prayer: We have told Him we wish our sins to be forgiven, but that He should only forgive them in the measure we forgive others.

Only the kind of love that comes from God willingly forgives sins and offenses against us. Remove God's love from the heart, and what is left? Hatred. And hatred does not know how, or even why, offenses should be forgiven. Where God's love is growing, however, a man or woman can forgive confidently, freely—not allowing themselves to worry over whether the offender should be made to pay in some way, or whether the offense will happen again. Worries like these close our hearts off from the operation of God's love.

Brothers and sisters, read the whole first epistle of John for yourselves—and see whether he recommends any other way to live or to handle offenses, other than by offering God's free and full love to all! We should never be concerned that we might remind each other "too much" about living in God's love, as if there is ever an end to it.

Therefore, never let the deep reality of God's love be absent from our hearts, no matter what is done to us—and never let love be absent in anything that we say to one another.

HOMILIES ON THE FIRST EPISTLE OF JOHN:1

My Father, as I dwell on the fullness of your forgiveness for me . . . paid for with the blood of your own Son . . . given freely to me . . . all my evil forgotten . . . give me a fresh deposit of quick forgiveness for others today.

Let forgiveness flow from me, quick and free, so that any offense against me is like a dead leaf fallen in a river— washing away in a moment.

27
Holy Spirit: Power of Love

Dear children, let us not love with words or tongue, but with actions and in truth. This, then, is how we know that we belong to the truth. . . .

—

1 John 3:18

*T*he Apostle Paul tells us, "God has poured out his love in our hearts by the Holy Spirit, whom he has given us" (Romans 5:5). We must lay hold of the truth that the Holy Spirit is at the center of all that is thought or done with the intention of loving with God's love.

Be assured that the Holy Spirit can never be poured out to men and women of wicked hearts, who are unwilling to love. Again and again, the Scriptures speak of Him as a spiritual "water" flowing from God, as in this case: "Let [your springs] be yours alone, never to be shared with strangers" (Proverbs 5:17). Those who do not love God are the strangers who are unable to "drink" the refreshing water of God's love, which is poured out within us by the Holy Spirit.

This is a hard saying, but it must be said: When we will not drink from the spiritual well of love—"God is love"—then we are acting in a spirit that was not given to us by Christ. And if it is not Christ's Spirit, then it is the spirit of antichrist.

It is true that any man or woman may come and go in the Church at will—but if they will not drink from the well of love they will not be counted among the children of God. A man who is empty of God's love may give a public declaration of faith by being baptized. He may even speak out the Word of God, or even prophesy. (As we read in 1 Samuel 19, Saul persecuted the innocent David, and all the while he was exercising the gift of prophecy!)

A man or woman who is inwardly wicked—without love, unforgiving, full of anger and hatred—can even take part in the sacrament of the body and blood of our Lord. In other words, they may call themselves a Christian.

Yes, someone may take part in all these outer "evidences" of faith. But to say that someone who allows wicked hatred in his heart also has God's love—this cannot be. The truth is, he knows nothing about God, or love. Beware!

Love, then, is the "gift" that brings us into greatest intimacy with God. Love alone is our spiritual well-spring. The Spirit of God calls to you and to me, "Come and drink!"

And with this invitation, the Spirit is even now inviting us to drink deeply of God himself.

HOMILIES ON THE FIRST EPISTLE OF JOHN:6

My Father, I can only bear these difficult words if I first come to you and "drink of your love"— hearing reassurances of your love for me, with all my weaknesses and failings.

Make me stronger by your love to me, so that I can live better with others, by your love through me. . . .

Today, let there be no "division" between my desire to be like you, and my actions toward the children, the men and the women you have given me to love.

28
The "Hands and Feet" Of Love

Follow the way of love.

1 Corinthians 14:1

*I*f you should seek God with the eyes of your soul, you will perhaps be tempted to imagine Him in certain ways.

Some may imagine they perceive Him as an immense warmth and brightness that is something *like* but infinitely greater than the sunlight when it floods over a vast, open landscape. Others may imagine they perceive Him in the form of an elderly man, dignified in wisdom and years.

Do not let yourself think of God like this, for you will be misled in your search for Him.

You should think only one thought, if you wish to perceive God and become like Him, day by day: "God is love."

What kind of face does love have? What shape and height? Does it have feet? Hands? We ought not limit God by thinking of Him like this.

Yet *love* has feet. For when our feet are "fitted with . . . the gospel of peace" (Ephesians 6:15), then love will be leading those who are lost and alone into the fellowship and grace that comes in the Church.

And love has hands. For when we love, we will use our hands to care privately for the poor (Matthew 6:3, 4).

Love also has eyes. For when our eyes are full of compassion, we quickly become aware of the needs of others. As the psalmist says, "Blessed is he who has regard for the weak" (Psalm 41:1).

And we know that love has ears. It was to the one who wants to grow in love that our Lord spoke when He said, "He who has ears to hear, let him hear" (Luke 8:8).

Dear brothers and sisters in Christ, why is it that when God's love for you is proclaimed in the congregation, you clap and shout joyfully? Is it just because you experience a sense of warmth and light inside? Is that all there is to love—a feeling, and not a force that causes us truly to care for men and women whom we can touch and see?

Please ponder this seriously. Have I ever talked to you about love as if it were a colored pigment you coat something with? Have I ever talked about it as if were a container, like an article made of gold or silver? No, love is the invisible presence of God with us (Isaiah 7:14, 15), teaching us within how to do right to each other.

If it pleases you to clap and shout for joy when you hear God's love for you declared, I say that is well and good! But if it excites you to praise His love in this way, then I hope you will be just as excited when I say love must be a force that is at work in your heart, leading you to serve each other.

HOMILIES ON THE FIRST EPISTLE OF JOHN:10

My Father, open my eyes to the hurts . . . the lostness . . . the brokenness all around me.

Today . . . who will you send to me that I can touch with your hands of kindness . . . comfort and encourage with your words of welcome and praise?

And who will you send me to seek, in wild and lost places?

29
Fire that Burns Also Brings Light

As for you, you were dead in your transgressions and sins. . . .

Ephesians 2:1

*W*hen the Lord sends His desolating coals, it is only to destroy what has been built in us for evil. When this place is cleared there rises the temple, a dwelling place, for the kind of happiness that flows out from eternity.

But I do not want you to miss what the psalmist means by referring to "coals" (Psalm 120:4).

To convert to the Lord is to pass from death to life. Before a coal is ignited, we might say it is still "dead." But when it is set afire it is a "live" coal. This is an excellent image of the change that takes place when a man or woman who is dead in sin is converted to the Lord.

Sometimes we hear people say, with surprise, "You should have seen him before—he was a heavy drinker, and his life was a shambles." Or "He loved the 'good life.' " Or "He was the biggest cheat I'd ever met!" And then they add, "I can hardly believe it now. He serves God so earnestly—and you know, there is this air of innocence about him. As if everything he did in the past had never happened."

Why the surprise? Because the sinner was a dead man, and now he is a live coal. Spiritual people, who know these eternal truths, may even have wept over this one, as mourners weep for the dead. But now they see him alive—and they overflow with joy!

There is something in this illustration that I want you to take for yourself.

We become excited and praise God whenever we see one of these "coals" catch fire. But if we are wise, we will eagerly seek out that thing in us that is still extinguished—by that I mean, anything within us that is slow to follow after God. Then bring it near one of these "coals" that has been set afire by God's Spirit.

And be ready and armed with the Word of God. To become converted, you must fight your way past the deceitful voice within.

HOMILIES ON THE PSALMS:5

Father, what is there in me that's still "unconverted"? What am I hiding from you? (As if I could hide anything. . .) Why am I afraid of giving over to you certain things I do . . . relationships . . . desires?

104

I know you are the only one who gives eternal life—but why am I afraid to give up things of this passing, fading life to you?

Help me to face and conquer the deceitful voice within—the voice that wants to excuse and justify the wrong in me. Let me see clearly all that is still dead coals . . . and then set fire to it.

30

Joy, the Promised Fruit

*He who goes out weeping, carrying seed to sow, will
return with songs of joy, carrying sheaves with him.*

Psalm 126:6

*T*his psalm—which speaks to the spirit of
those who are determined to continue in their spiritual journey toward God—is perfectly suited to
helping us in times of sorrow and longing. This
world is, without doubt, a valley of tears where one
sows while weeping.

It will help you to continue on in your faith,
however, if I explain what this Scripture means by
the "seeds" we are to sow.

They are the good works, which God has created for each of us to do (Ephesians 2:10). And He
has planned that we are to accomplish them, by the
power of His Spirit, in the very midst of this troubled, tumultuous life.

Whoever learns to do God's work well in this

world—this valley of tears and troubles—becomes hearty, like the sturdy farmer who sows seed even in the dead of winter. Do cold winds, or harsh weather prevent him from working? Not at all!

Thus we should see the troubles of this world as they are: diversions thrown in our path by the evil one, meant to turn us away from the good works we are created to do. See what the psalmist says: "He who goes out weeping. . . ." We will indeed find cause for weeping, every one of us. And yet we must go, doing the good works of God on our way.

How miserable if we were called to work so hard and *only* to weep, without seeing any fruit for our work. How miserable if there were no one to wipe away our tears.

But we know that some operation of the Spirit is at work, when we continue sowing even in our tears. For the Spirit promises, through the psalmist, that we will return—astonished with joy!—and carrying the fruit of our labor as an offering to Him.

HOMILIES ON THE PSALMS:2

My Father, how thankful I am that you are always active in "good works" toward me. I can never repay your goodness to me.

And all that you ask is that I not tire of doing what's right, no matter how unresponsive the heart of some

107

whom you've called me to serve. Only you can give me strength and courage today, because you know where the way is rugged.

Fix my sights on the coming harvest of joy!

31
Becoming a Wise Servant

I lift up my eyes to you, to you whose throne is in heaven. As the eyes of slaves look to the hand of their master, as the eyes of a maid look to the hand of her mistress, so our eyes look to the Lord our God, till he shows us his mercy.

Psalm 123:2

*T*hese psalms that are called "songs of ascent" teach us how to "ascend" and progress in our walk with God.

By the Spirit, the psalmist is calling us to ascend in heart—that is, to increase in the right kind of holy desire, which is something more than seeking after "spiritual feelings."

We start with faith, believing in the reality of God's unseen world and the enduring principles of His kingdom. This kindles within us a lively hope that we are children of the kingdom. And this, in turn, causes us to pour out God's love on others—

all of which increases our desire to experience the eternal presence of God *now*, as well as in the life to come, which is without end. That is how we "ascend."

I am speaking to you from this Scripture because you are dismayed at a warning you have read in the Gospel—a certain passage that sounds as if God is making terrible threats against you. You have read that the Day of the Lord will come like a thief in the night. As Jesus said, in a parable, "If the owner of the house had known at what time of night the thief was coming, he would have kept watch and would not have let his house be broken into. So you must also be ready. . ." (Matthew 24:43, 44).

In your dismay and fear you think, "How can anyone be prepared for Him if the hour will come like a thief? Isn't this unfair?"

First, I say to you, it is *because* you don't know the hour of His coming that you should be vigilant in faith, constantly. Perhaps God has actually planned it this way, keeping us ignorant of the hour of His coming so that we might be ready for Him each moment—the way a slave looks to the hand of his master.

This "hour" will be a surprise to those who consider themselves "master of their own house"—by which Jesus means men who proudly govern their affairs without considering the will of their true master. Therefore, don't be a "master" in this false way, and you won't be surprised and dismayed.

You ask me, "Then what shall I be like?"

Be like the man you have heard about from the psalmist who cried, "I am poor and afflicted" (Psalm 68:30, Douay).

If you see that you are always poor and afflicted in spirit (Matthew 5:3), then your eyes will ever be upon the Lord, and you will receive the mercy that both comforts and gives you strength to continue.

HOMILIES ON THE PSALMS:3

My Father, have you already come to me—as someone in need of attention, concern, help—and I failed to see that it was you?

Lord, before I run off to "make things right" on my own, let me always listen for your wise word . . . so that I speak and act and serve, not in my human guilt, but in your goodness and strength.

32
Our New Source of Life

Dear friends, do not believe every spirit, but test the spirits to see whether they are from God . . . every spirit that does not acknowledge Jesus is not from God. This is the spirit of antichrist, which you have heard is coming and even now is already in the world. You, dear children, are from God and have overcome them, because greater is he that is in you . . .

1 John 4:1, 3, 4

We know that whoever "divides" Jesus Christ—denying that He was both God and Man—is not of God.

But we have also explained to you, as you recall, that it is possible to "divide" Jesus Christ in another way. Everyone who violates God's love, is in effect denying that Jesus Christ has come in the flesh. For there was no other reason that Jesus came in a physical body, except to demonstrate the pouring out of God's love for flesh-and-blood men.

This powerful love, which I keep recommending to you, is nothing other than what Jesus Christ himself recommends to you in the Gospel: "Greater love has no one than this, that one lay down his life for his friends. You are my friends if you do what I command" (John 15:13).

Whoever violates love—by thinking or acting hatefully toward any single man, woman or child—denies Christ by his life. Even if he *thinks* he believes Jesus has come in the flesh, and even if he *confesses with his lips* Jesus has come in the flesh—if he does not love, he divides Christ. If this is the case, the spirit of antichrist is at work in him, wherever he is, wherever he goes.

But what did John say to those who are citizens of the "Fatherland," for which we so deeply long? "You have overcome them"—meaning those who carry the spirit of antichrist.

Who are we speaking of? How shall we identify them?

They are the ones who speak the "wise" language of this world. I will say it plainly, you will know them because they speak against God's love.

You have heard the Lord say, "If you forgive men when they sin against you, your heavenly Father will also forgive you" (Matthew 6:14). When our Lord spoke these words, He was either telling us the truth, or He was lying. If you are a Christian and say you believe Christ, you must also accept the authority of this truth, spoken by one who said, "I am the truth" (John 14:6).

Now compare what He has said with the language of this world: "What! You're not going to take revenge, after what was done to you? Why, he'll go around boasting, telling everyone what a weakling you are for letting him get away with his offense. Don't be a fool. Show him who he is dealing with."

Only those who love the world say such things. And only those who still love the world listen to them.

Lest this word weigh heavily upon you and not encourage you on in the Lord—which is what I intend—I add this quickly: We *are* of God. How can I be sure of this?

Whoever hears this teaching and is not of God, it will be to him as nothing at all. It won't touch or affect him in any way. But whoever is born of God will feel a prick in his heart because of what I have just been saying. Only the ones who have the Spirit of Truth, may hear what the Spirit is saying in their heart.

This is to encourage you. So let us go on choosing to listen to John, who advises us in the Spirit of Truth.

HOMILIES ON THE FIRST EPISTLE OF JOHN:2, 3

My Father, show me the false well-springs I've been trying to draw my life from . . . accomplishments . . . possessions . . . abilities. . . .

Help me to see that when I rely on these things as my

114

source of well-being and worth, I will always act in anger when someone threatens.

But I am of God! Born of you . . . alive in you! No one can threaten my place in you. Nothing in you can be taken from me. I am not hindered, but free. . . .

33
An "Upward" Destiny

Jesus also suffered and died outside the city's gate in order that He might purify and consecrate the people through the shedding of His own blood, and set them apart as holy—for God. Let us go forth, from all that would prevent us, to Him outside the camp. . . . For here we have no permanent city, but we are looking for the one which is to come.

Hebrews 13:12–14, Amplified

I want it to be clear and fixed in your minds, that there are two possible destinies for man. This is part of God's appointed plan for us, and it cannot be avoided, even by those who invent all manner of new philosophies.

It is not by accident that men work so hard, inventing so many different philosophies and reasonings as to how a man may live a happy and fulfilled life in the midst of this unhappy world. I myself have worked hard to understand their philosophies, so that I might speak wisely to unbe-lievers. My hope is that what we Christians know about the eternal—by personal, inner revelation from God's Spirit—might be revealed to unbeliev-ers by logic and reason. I long to show them how different is their vain thinking (which of course leads to a vain way of living), from the hope God gives us—a hope that brings into this life the true happiness we're seeking, which comes only from God!

Notice how the worldly thinkers—and anyone who thinks like them—will wind up in endless ar-guments about the "ultimate good" and the "ulti-mate evil." All the while they are trying to discover what manner of thinking and living will allow men to live in a state of perfect happiness. But they have chosen the wrong starting point.

What is the secret then, that will cause us to live in perfect peace and contentment, no matter what circumstances prevail? What is man's "ultimate good" in this earthly life?

It is to live with our eyes on the goal—the prize of our faith, the upward calling—to a celestial City of God, which shines up ahead, high above us. When we fix the eye of our soul upon this "city on a hill" (Matthew 5:14–16), the joy and longing to reach its bright walls causes us to lay aside every earthly weight (Hebrews 12:1). Its shining light of truth becomes our inner government, regulating all that we do, so that we make wise and good choices. If we follow this light, it will keep us from turning off the path into dark byways, so that we delay in reaching the goal, or miss it altogether.

So it is this sense of an upward destiny that must be fulfilled for its own sake—the capacity created within us to be imitators of God (Ephesians 5:1). All other ways of living will leave us ever empty, and searching, as if we are still among the lost.

I must also tell you that this bright City of God—which beckons us and is, at the same time, being formed in us—is not reached during this life in the sense that we can reach an earthly city. It is not a spiritual state of "perfection" in which we can say, "I've done enough good works, so I can sit down and rest now." No, it is that state of relying on God continuously, so that we are walking, acting and speaking what is perfect and good.

CITY OF GOD:1

My Father, who lives in eternity, what "weight" will you help me shed today?

How am I blinded from seeing the light of your "City" . . . by an ambition . . . the hunger for a possession . . . by trying to find my life in a human love?

Like one who is blind, or possessed by an evil—heal the eyes of my soul, and cast this weight off me today!

I lift my renewed eyes now, to look upon the beauty of your holiness!

34
Four "Traps" of the Soul

Surely the day is coming, it will burn like a furnace.
All the arrogant and every evildoer will be stubble,
and that day that is coming will set them on fire, says
the Lord Almighty . . .
But for you who revere my name, the sun of
righteousness will rise with healing in its wings. And
you will go out and leap like calves
released from the stall.

Malachi 4:1, 2

*T*here are four things that all men naturally seek, instinctively, without prompting by anyone. They are:

Pleasure—that is, moments when we experience agreeable, physical sensations.

Relaxation—by which I mean the absence of inner stresses as well as physical labors. (Often we seek both of these together.)

Good health—including safety, along with free-

119

dom from illness, disease and infirmity.

Ease of the soul—by which I mean, relief from oppressions such as are common to natural men, like depression, sorrow, anger.

These four drives are so strong within us that in order to make any spiritual progress, we must actively cultivate our soul so that it will grow in godly virtues. Growth in spirit will never happen naturally, being overshadowed by these other powerful, all-consuming desires.

And yet, it is our desire to grow in the character of God that must rule over all. Otherwise, the body and soul of man will always have dominance over the virtues that recreate us in the image of God. I need only to give you one example of this, knowing you will quickly see what I mean and be able to apply it to the other three pursuits as well.

Consider bodily pleasure, and in particular, sexual intercourse. When the desire to grow in godly virtue rules in our lives, then sexual intercourse is enjoyed for its own sake—but is also governed by higher considerations. By that I mean, we take into account the responsibility we bear if a child is created by our union.

But what happens when a man thinks only of pleasure, and not godly virtue? The truth is, men conveniently choose between these two all the time—sometimes excusing their behavior by saying there is "nothing wrong with natural drives." While on many other issues (when it suits their cause), they loudly demand that their way be based

120

on "higher spiritual values."

And so, many men and women have fooled themselves into thinking that virtue—the pursuit of godliness—should always be subject to their own pleasure. They only uphold those spiritual values that allow them to seek their own pleasure. This is a deformed kind of life. For physical pleasure, ungoverned, is a tyrant. And the kind of so-called "higher spiritual value" that is subject to pleasure is no spiritual value at all.

Sadly, this kind of thinking holds sway among many popular thinkers—and has no end of patrons and defenders among common men. . . .

Doubtless, there are many who become waylaid and lost on their spiritual journey toward God. They make this same mistake—believing that what they desire is their own "highest good," whether it be relaxation, good health, or ease of soul.

CITY OF GOD:1, 2

Father of Truth—my Rescuing Shepherd!—I open the gates of my heart to you. Wage war in me, to rescue me from the wrong beliefs and false goals that hold me captive. . . .

I leap at the freedom you offer! I run to you from the shadows I see within me—to you, my risen sun of righteousness!

35
The Spirit Wars Against the Flesh

Grace and peace be yours in abundance through the knowledge of God and of Jesus our Lord. His divine power has given us everything we need for life and godliness through our knowledge of him who called us by his own glory and goodness. Through these he has given us his very great and precious promises, so that through them you may participate in the divine nature and escape the corruption in the world caused by evil desires.

2 Peter 1:2-4

I have been talking to you about virtue—that is, living according to godly standards, which are known to us as "high truths." Living this way does not happen naturally, but comes by spiritual growth, little by little, as we hear and act on sound teaching from wise and godly men.

Now I want you to know something about trying to live according to the Spirit.

The man or woman who determines to live a godly life will find themselves in a constant struggle—sometimes more subtle, sometimes more obvious and overwhelming. The great difficulty is that they find themselves involved in a war that is not external but internal. Sometimes it will seem like they are warring against an evil agency that attacks from outside themselves. But most often, it will be clear that they are fighting against an evil tendency that has sunk its roots into their own nature.

This war is waged especially when a person tries to check the lusts of the flesh. Immediately, they find that these lusts begin to appeal to and weaken the mind through evil reasoning. The mind that does not know how to combat such an attack will justify wrong, until eventually it will give in to any crime against the Spirit and against God.

We must never think that we have totally escaped this evil warfare, as if we have attained such spiritual heights that we can never be attacked again. As the Apostle Paul says, "The desires of the flesh are opposed to the Holy Spirit, and the desires of the Spirit are opposed to Godless human nature; for these are continually in conflict with each other . . ." (Galatians 5:17, Amplified).

Nonetheless, we are to set our will to grow in goodness, with an eye on the high goal of being made perfect in love. This is the highest kind of goodness we can reach for in this world. Once we determine that this is our spiritual path, however—what can we expect?

The flesh will launch its secret war, and will begin "lusting" after the spirit. By that I mean, the fleshly forces will hunger and cry to be satisfied. These forces tell us it is right to satisfy every urge we may have—even if it means dragging someone else away from the path of godliness, to the harm of their soul, and even if it means letting ourselves wander from the upward path of godliness.

So when we are warned by the apostle, he means for us to beware at all times. For there are forces within that want to violate what is high and good and pure and beautiful. In this lifetime, we cannot escape this warfare, no matter how much we desire to be free of it.

I tell you all of this so you will not be dismayed and give up when you find yourself in the midst of struggle. Who is there so wise and sinlessly perfect that he has won final, ultimate victory over this war between flesh and spirit?

We can, however, achieve this much with God's help: We can learn how to rightly restrain the soul, so it will not give in to the voice of the flesh that woos. We can stand firm, and refuse to listen to its evil reasonings and justifications.

We can refuse to give in and make even the first step toward sin.

THE CITY OF GOD:4

124

My Father, am I sometimes my own worst enemy? Do I give up and give in, just when you are about to give me the victory?

I set my mind on . . . patience . . . honesty . . . kindness . . . goodness . . . gentleness . . . love . . . all the qualities that describe you . . .

. . . so that your Spirit may walk in the silent depths of me today . . . may breathe through my words . . . be present to others through all that I do.

36
Vigilance Against Evil

[Because of] the corruption in this world caused by evil desires . . . make every effort to add to your faith goodness; and to goodness [add] knowledge; and to knowledge [add] self-control; and to self-control [add] perseverance. . . .

2 Peter 1:4, 5

What should I tell you about the quality known as *prudence*? It means, *to be vigilant at all times in discerning between what is good and evil*. We must have this kind of discernment if we are to continue on the upward path spiritually, and not fall into sin.

When we are vigilant, we learn to become aware of the moment when we begin consenting to sinful thoughts, which soon lead to sinful actions. Then we are able to fight back the attack.

And then there is the quality men know as *temperance*. Temperance is *the spiritual strength by which we cut sinful thoughts and desires from us—as if by use of a blade that has been strengthened by fire.*

CITY OF GOD:4

My Father, my heart is full of gratitude that you ever watch over me. Because you live outside of time, you know when temptation is aimed at me . . .

Deliver me from evil! Set a guard around my heart . . . upon my lips. . . .

With the sword of the Spirit, which is your Word, let me separate myself from sin by your Spirit.

Cut evil from me!—so I can walk on freely with you. . . .

37
God Is at Work for Us

We know that as long as we are at home in the body we are away from the Lord. . . . We are confident [that we belong to God, as His children], and would prefer to be away from the body and at home with the Lord. So we make it our goal to please him. . . . For we must all appear before the judgment seat of Christ, that each one may receive what is due him for the things done while in the body, whether good or bad.

2 Corinthians 5:6–10

The Gospel of Christ . . . is God's power working unto salvation . . . to everyone who believes with a personal trust and a constant surrender and firm reliance. . . . For in the Gospel a righteousness . . . is revealed, both springing from faith and leading to faith. . . . As it is written, "The man who through faith is just and upright shall live, and shall live by faith."

Romans 1:16, 17, Amplified; Habakkuk 2:4, Amplified

*T*here is much you need to know about the godly quality, or virtue, that we call *justice*.

Justice, in one sense, is this: *the task of assigning to each man what is due to him in the end, according to his achievements.*

And yet, we must come to justice in its other sense. There exists in man a definite understanding of the natural and right order of things. When man lives according to this inner sense of God's right order, then his soul is under the governance of God. Then, too, his flesh comes under the governance of his soul. All this results in a peace and sense of balance, because both flesh and soul are in accord with God's order.

This too is justice, and it is a state that we labor in the spirit to reach. Doesn't the fact that we often struggle against God's order bear witness that our flesh is still warring against the Spirit? And—more hopeful—doesn't this struggle also bear witness that God's Spirit is still laboring with us, that is to say He is laboring *for* us, working to bring us under God's divine order?

The fact that this godly quality—an active justice—brings a struggle within is a good sign. It means God has not pronounced final judgment, but is still working to make us "right with him."

When we think that we are "justified" in the ultimate sense—as if we can stop laboring in spirit—then we fall into danger. We stop being mindful of God and His ways, and so our soul gradually steps out from under the rule of God. Then the soul grows weaker, and the flesh begins to win more and more of its unrelenting attacks. Fleshly hungers of all kinds prevail.

Therefore, as long as we are beleaguered by the army of fleshly hungers—this plague of desires, this sickness!—how can we dare to say that we are "saved"? How dare we act as if all is at peace when we are at war, and not blessed with the final happiness, which is release from all sin into God's presence?

CITY OF GOD:4

My Father: Who will govern my life today? Me—or you?

Help me to choose wisely, moment by moment. . . .

38
The "Order" of Love

By him [Jesus], all things were created. . . . He is before all things, and in him all things hold together. And he is the head of the body, the church; he is the beginning and the firstborn from among the dead, so that in everything he might have the supremacy . . . by making peace through his blood, shed on the cross.

Colossians 1:16–20

Make every effort to live in peace with all men and to be holy; without holiness no one will see the Lord.

Hebrews 12:14

*F*or now, we are pilgrims. We are away from our God for a time, yet bound for His eternal Celestial City (Revelation 21), walking by the kind of faith that holds fast to the inner vision of what we shall be when He appears (1 John 3:2), though we cannot see with human eyes the goal of our faith.

The tendency of our natural soul is to seek peace—but it must be the kind of peace that is under the order and governance of God, or it is no real peace at all. Any other kind of peace that we seek—whether in leisurely rest, or in mental distractions—will eventually fail. As pilgrims—that is, mortals who are seeking our eternal home with an immortal God—we reach across into the eternal by bringing our souls under the "order" of God, living in obedience to His eternal laws which uphold all things and cannot be changed.

God, whom we must think of at all times as our Master, has taught us two foundational truths about the way eternal peace will come into our lives: Love God first. Love your neighbor, as you love yourself. Living in this way fulfills the law of God (Matthew 22:37–39).

Take note of the order that exists within our Master's teaching.

The man or woman who loves God *first* will find himself living the good kind of life—growing in godly qualities—that brings about his own highest good. When he is living like this, it can be said that a man truly loves himself, and is free from worry, fear and self-centeredness, finally at peace within himself.

As a result of finding this inner peace of God, he becomes truly at rest (Hebrews 4:1–13). Then, free from self-concern, his concern extends to his neighbor: that his neighbor should come to love God and find this same peace and freedom.

There is one other step in this godly order. A man should wish his neighbor to show concern for him also, if he is in need, and to receive help when it is offered.

As we live according to this order, we will fulfill the law of God. We will find ourselves living—so far as it is possible in the limitations of human society—at peace with all men. While we are here in this earthly city, then, live according to these simple but eternal truths that come from the Celestial City:

Do not hurt anyone, in body or in spirit.

As far as you are able, help everyone.

THE CITY OF GOD:14

Father, so often I get weary, and fail to do the good thing. Sometimes I don't offer to help, when it's in my power to make things a little easier for someone.

I want to be in your "order" of love today!

So I come to you first, Father, my Well-spring of all that is Good. I rest in you. Fill me with the depths of compassion that are in you, so that love will flow down into this mean and sullen and needy world from your eternal kingdom. . . .

39
Love Family First

If anyone does not provide for his relatives, and especially for his immediate family, he has denied the faith and is worse than an unbeliever.

———

1 Timothy 5:8

For the unbelieving husband is set apart (separated, withdrawn from heathen contamination and affiliated with Christian people) by union with his consecrated (set-apart) wife; and the unbelieving wife is set apart and separated through union with her consecrated husband.

———

1 Corinthians 7:14, Amplified

We are commanded to love our neighbor as ourselves. Therefore, a man's first duty under God's order is to love his wife and children. In saying this, I want to make sure you know that a man's primary responsibility—and a woman's also—is to those in their own household.

Since God established this order in humanity itself—husbands, wives and children—it stands to reason that we must fulfill the law of love at home first. After all, who else has more opportunity to "test" our love and peace and patience than those we live with? And whom else should we seek to love first, besides those we can most readily and easily serve?

Yes, we may provide all else for our families, in terms of material comforts and possessions, but if we fail to provide God's love for them, the Apostle Paul shows us our true hearts—worse than infidels! And yet, he says this to waken our understanding that God desires heavenly peace to rule in our homes, flowing from those who are placed in charge *in love* to those who are called to obey *in love*.

Therefore, in governing our homes, the one who gives commands should only do so out of godly concern—not from hard-heartedness, or with the kind of authority that has no understanding or compassion. This is the gentle manner in which direction and godly strength is to be given— from husband to wife, parents to children, and to anyone else involved in your household.

In the home of the just—that is, the one who is living by faith, as a pilgrim headed toward the Celestial City—those who give direction and commands are actually serving those whom they seem to command. Their motive for governing at home should not be to dominate, but because they are rightly concerned for the spiritual well-being and growth of the others.

Therefore, as you exercise your authority, do not fall into pride because of your "position." Rather, exercise your spiritual authority in your family, being ruled yourself by God's love—which encourages, hopes, believes, and never fails (1 Corinthians 13).

City of God:14

Father, where those of my "household" are weak or unbelieving in any way—whether spouse or children or others—work through me to "set them apart." Give me depths of faith and love, so they may see your light in me and step out of darkness and unbelief into a new trust in you.

Father, help me not to "govern" out of stubborn strength, or mere ego. Give me the spiritual authority that comes from living in union with you, so that the rule of your kingdom may come upon my family.

40
Peace, Rest and Joy for the Children of God

But you have come to Mount Zion, to the heavenly Jerusalem, the city of the Living God. You have come to thousands upon thousands of angels in joyful assembly, to the church of the firstborn, whose names are written in heaven. You have come to God, the judge of all men, to the spirits of righteous men made perfect, to Jesus the mediator of a new covenant, and to the sprinkled blood that speaks a better word. . . . Therefore, since we are receiving a kingdom that cannot be shaken, let us be thankful, and so worship God acceptably with reverence and awe, for our God is a consuming fire.

Hebrews 12: 22–24, 28, 29

---

*T*he highest good that flows from, and leads to the City of God is the promise of everlasting peace—all things reconciled and in order under the love of God.

It is not the kind of peace that natural men encounter, simply by experiencing moments without turmoil which occur for us all between birth and death. No, it is the peace in which immortals dwell. In this eternal peace—not of ourselves but which we hold within, like golden containers—we do not suffer at all from external adversities, no matter how difficult.

Who can deny that this is the most deeply joyful kind of life that can be lived in this present world?

Who would dare to compare such a life lived under the sheltering peace of God with anything this world can offer? There is no real security in possessions, no matter how much you own. And there is no real tranquility in mental exercises and leisure pursuits, no matter how much they "dull" our perception that there is still an eternal judge whom we must face. All of these false pursuits of peace are wretched.

And yet . . .

Whoever lives this life for the sake of that life to come, he will find peace.

Be sure that the flame of your love for the heavenly City of God continues to burn brighter. Likewise, fix your hopes on your heavenly destination. Though others will surely call you absurd, you will know in your heart that they are the fools who will not enter into the unshakable peace that comes from God and leads us to Him.

The false happiness and security offered by this life is good for the wise, but it will never lead the unwise to God. Quite the contrary, the earthly mind does not know how to use godly values when faced with earthly circumstances. Therefore, earthly-minded men will not know how to *judge* between good and evil, nor will they choose to act courageously against what is wrong, and will always be controlled by small, dark and self-serving actions.

But you are different.

You have set your heart toward a different goal. You have set your eyes upon the all-encompassing God, who will *be* all *in* all (1 Corinthians 15:28). You have fixed your course by determining to live for eternity.

Continue to live with this high goal in view, and you will remain in perfect peace.

CITY OF GOD:20

*F*ather *of Peace, I praise and thank you for sending into my life Jesus, the Prince of Peace.*

Thank you for setting before me the highway to your City . . . which is love. . . .

And thank you that, in all things that may come my way—whether calm or turmoil, the irritation or kindness of another—you will give me the strength to respond . . . with peace that comes to me from heaven!

DAVID HAZARD developed the "Rekindling the Inner Fire" devotional series to encourage others to keep the "heart" of their faith alive and afire with love for God. He also feels a special need to help Christians of today to "meet" men and women of the past whose experience of God belongs to the whole Church, for all the ages.

Hazard is an award-winning writer, the author of books for both adults and children, with international bestsellers among his many titles. He lives in northern Virginia with his wife, MaryLynne, and three children: Aaron, Joel, and Sarah Beth.